John Lockwood

The River

A Song of Human Life

John Lockwood

The River
A Song of Human Life

ISBN/EAN: 9783337374846

Printed in Europe, USA, Canada, Australia, Japan

Cover: Foto ©Thomas Meinert / pixelio.de

More available books at **www.hansebooks.com**

THE RIVER:

A SONG OF HUMAN LIFE.

By ALA,

Author of "The Silent Dormitory and Other Poems," "Disciple-
ship," "The Two Paths," etc.

PRIVATELY PRINTED IN HONOR OF OUR MOTHER'S
NINETY-FOURTH BIRTHDAY.

JOHN LOCKWOOD,
138-140 SOUTH OXFORD STREET,
BROOKLYN, N. Y.,
1890.

WHAT IF SHE NE'ER RETURN!

Mother is gone ; her empty chair I see,
    Gone! but, please God, she cometh soon again.
O joy! she cometh back again to me.
    What if she ne'er return ! To her, sweet gain,
    To me immeasurable loss and pain.
I dare not think of that distressful day
    When from the window I shall gaze in vain
For her returning steps, unwont to stray,
That come no more, howe'er with breaking heart I pray.

THE RIVER:

A SONG OF HUMAN LIFE.

THE RIVER : A SONG OF HUMAN LIFE.

Out of a dingle wild

I came, dear Nature's child,

A brooklet undefiled,

    As crystal clear.

I danced to see the light

Of the pure heaven so bright,

And sparkled at the sight

    Of sunbeams near.

Out of the great mystery, the Human Soul is ushered into the world, at birth, in immaculate innocence and perfect beauty.

Shot by the sun's strong bow,

They pierced me through and through—

'T was but their way to show

   Their welcome sweet.

By mossy rocks I played,

'Twixt banks of fern I strayed,

In cozy nooks delayed

   My baby-feet.

Absorbing mother-love greets it, and it soon finds its way to the delights which kindly Nature has provided for it on every side.

There laughing zephyrs came

Breathing love's blissful name,

But innocent of shame

   I heeded not :

With gleeful strife and din

They pressed my cheeks and chin,

They pressed love-dimples in,

   Then kissed the spot.

Being wholly unacquainted with sin, the babe is unaffected by its approaches.

Unmoved to love's delay

Eftsoons I slipped away,

For I would be at play

    Amid my toys:

The pebbles at my feet,

Whereon as harpchords sweet

I swept my fingers fleet,

    Sang of my joys.

Impatient of dalliance, it seeks its playthings with glee, and coos its innocent happiness.

Lured by my dancing wave,

For me the wild-bird gave

His wood-notes gay and grave

    In shade and shine ;

Swinging from tree to tree,

So fearless and so free,

The squirrel played for me

    His antics fine.

Finding in Nature a response to every desire, it
more and more seeks her sympathetic companion-
ship.

Unto my pebbly brink

Came creatures wild to drink—

Duck, otter, weasel, mink—

And plash and play :

Happy betwixt my banks,

I watched their brimming pranks,

And heard their noisy thanks

The livelong day.

Pets are drawn to the child, who is in turn attracted
to them.

By pool and waterfall,

By rapids great and small,

I heard the red fox call

    His loitering mate.

I heard the panther's growl,

I heard the lone wolf's howl,

I heard the midnight owl

    Hoot his " Too late ! "

With observant eyes the child gradually gets acquainted with its sweet companion, Nature,

By many a soft cascade

Whose melody delayed

Whatever footsteps strayed

    Within their spells,

By many a grassy bed

With strawberries white and red

And violets interspread

    And lily-bells,

and with advancing years grows in sweetness and
beauty;

There poets loitered long

My rocks and rills among

And caught a loftier song—

    Diviner fire :

There lovers came to find

In me a purer mind,

An essence more refined

    Than love's desire.

and begins to get glimpses of the deeper significance
and beauty and purity of the world.

Thus many a day and mile

My life was one sweet smile,

With naught that could defile

My earth-pure stream :

Nor shadows that oft creep

O'er life's serenest sleep

Came to disturb my deep

And golden dream.

It begins to perceive that it has a share in the untainted splendor of the universe,

At length not far away,

Where slept the sun all day,

I found a meadow gay

    With daffodils :

There the lush grass was green,

And there the floral sheen

Lay beautiful between

    The sun-kissed hills.

and enters completely into the enjoyment of the

There children golden-tressed,

By sunbeams soft caressed,

All day the cool grass pressed

    With knees and feet.

With them fond zephyrs played

And round their lips delayed :

O who could them upbraid ?—

    So pure, so sweet !

innocent loveliness of the world.

I watched them, boys and girls,

Their locks in tangled whorls

Of dandelion curls,

   That fairies know;

And they wore coronets

Of braided violets

More beautiful than frets

   A royal brow.

Nature, the indulgent mother, companions the spot-
less and beautiful

Their necklaces were made

Of buttercups abraid,

With clover leaves inlaid—

Ah, pretty weeds !

What they called " cheeses " round

On hollyhocks they found,

And these with grass they bound

To make them beads.

child of her bosom, inducting it into her mysteries

They chased with footsteps sly

And bonnets poised on high

The painted butterfly—

    That wingéd flower;

Till, hushed their noisy glee,

Beneath some spreading tree

Gave up each little knee

    To slumber's hour.

of innocent happiness.

Of this fair spot possessed

I loitered long at rest

Nor had within my breast

    Or thought or care.

I let my music die,

Content, stagnant, to lie

And gaze into the sky

    With vacant stare.

Passive to these influences it becomes enervated, not having yet discovered that it has a positive and commanding work of its own to do.

By scarce-seen affluents new,

Fed by the rain and dew,

More and more strong I grew ;

But lo, there crept

But conscience not having yet awakened, the child
knows nothing of sin, and so has not learned to be
on its guard against temptation.   From a mixed

Out of obscurity

Rills of impurity,

While in security

Fancied I slept.

environment, evil influences approach it along with
good ones, and the soul is contaminated, though yet
sinless, before it is aware.

Then on my garments' sheen

A track of stain was seen ;

Behold I was unclean !

Not quite in vain

Conscience awakens, and reason begins to discrimi-
nate between worthy and unworthy objects of pur-
suit. Fruits which reason has disapproved are

The pitying sun looked down,

(For this he hath his crown),

To cleanse my baby gown

Of this first stain.

tasted, and the taint of sin follows. This taint the
just-awakened spiritual force of the soul strives to
remove.

But more and more—O shame !—

Turbid my stream became ;

Matters not whose the blame,

Mine was the cross.

Sorrow follows condemnation, but it is not deep
enough to enable the soul to resist triumphantly the
allurements of pleasure ; nor is the understanding
yet sufficiently enlightened to give proper weight to

O this vile influence !

O this base indolence !

Lost was my innocence—

     Ah me ! the loss !

---

the dangers of temptation, and thus the soul's purity
is more and more stained with sin. Innocence is
gone for ever.

Near this sweet glade I found

A mill whereat I ground

For all the farmers round

Their golden grain.

But under the action of the mighty forces now at work, the understanding developes rapidly, the will takes command, defensive works are erected at the weak points, and the soul, fortified and guarded against surprise, is secure. The youth begins to see

More and more wheels beside

I turned with my swift tide,

And heard the shuttles glide

With might and main.

that he has a place in the great world's work, the
voice of Duty is heard and obeyed, and in the hum
of industry the calls of the tempting siren, though
heard, are unheeded.

Then on I ran in haste,

With all my waters waste,

My turbid stream more chaste

    For good work done ;

My dreams 'mid rocks and rills,

With babes and daffodils,

My service in the mills

    All past and gone.

Useful occupation gives the spiritual forces a chance to cleanse the soul, which now bids farewell to self-indulgence, frivolity, and idle dreaming, and even to the rougher forms of industrial activity,

By quiet farms I swept,

By hamlets still that slept,

By villages I crept,

     And on and on.

I heard the lambs repeat

Their soft, heart-touching bleat

Beneath the fervid heat

     Of summer's sun.

and enters, with a due sense of its allotted part, upon

I heard the piping quail,

I heard the black crow rail,

And, near, the threshing-flail

    On the barn floor.

The hovering hawk I saw—

A king whose might is law—

Eying with hungry maw

    The barnyard o'er.

life's momentous work.

Down to my brimming brink

Came flock and herd to drink,

And birds to preen and prink

    Their plumage gay.

I made the cool morass

Where in the tall, coarse grass

The cattle loved to pass

    Half the hot day.

The noble youth becomes a helper to those less able, a creator of beneficent instrumentalities,

The sun-loved golden grain,

Faint with my long disdain,

With the cool lips of the rain

   At length I kissed.

Also, the tryst to renew,

I sent my daughters true,

Soft-footed fog and dew

   And shrouding mist.

———

though at first, from mental preoccupation, consider-
ed cold and distant.

In a cradle of silk the corn

Has nestled since it was born,

And the silk will never be torn

   Till the grain be ripe.

The farmer will ne'er take his ease

Till he 's gathered the golden fleece ;

When his granary full he sees,

   He lights his pipe.

His industry bears rich fruit ;

He quietly ridges his brows

As he sees his well-stuffed mows,

And thinks of his good milch-cows

　In the winter's cold.

He opens and looks in his bins,

He slams them shut and grins,

And chuckles under his chins

　At sight of his gold.

he prospers and is glad.

Now I have ships that glide

Forth and far on my tide,

And I feel the pulse of the wide,

Majestic sea ;

And cities crowd to my shore,

Where money-kings sit in the door

Of their tents of smoke, whose roar

Comes ever to me.

He engages in trade and commerce, founds cities, and becomes a money-king.

I give the breath of my tide

To the atmosphere, my bride,

And away to the north it doth ride

On the southwind's wings.

Then it falls in a gentle rain

To nourish the thirsty grain,

And quickly joins me again

In the rills and springs.

His beneficent influence extends far and wide.

In the dusk the fisherman sets

In my current deep his nets,

And patiently awaits

     Dawn o'er the hills ;

Then he draws his nets, and behold !

Up from my waters cold

What beauties ! good as gold ;

     And his boat he fills.

His touch awakens the correlated forces of healthful
business activity,

Quick to the city streets

Come up the fishing fleets,

And them the huckster greets

   With a laugh in his sides ;

Then the huckster hawks my fish,

And the poor child hath its wish,

And shouts at the smoking dish

   The River provides.

and brings to the community the blessings of pros-
perity and happiness.

At anchor there in my bay

Are ships from lands far away

Across the sea and the day,

    With treasures unguessed.

The ships will be laden again

With riches of mountain and plain,

And, home-going pigeons, amain

    Will fly to their nest.

His ships sail every sea,

With these my shuttles of trade

The Cloth of Gold I braid,

Whose beauty never shall fade ;

That shall cover the world—

The Gospel of Love and Peace,

Whose jubilance never shall cease,

Whose banners shall float in the breeze,

Ne'er to be furled.

sowing in distant lands the seeds of universal frater-
nity, and teaching and spreading over the whole
earth the gospel of peace and good-will to men.

And now my goal is won;

The River's work, begun

In the far hills, is done;

The bar is passed.

Cleansed by thy purity,

O all-embracing sea,

I am absorbed in thee,

Rest! rest! at last.

Old age comes on at last, crowned with success and peaceful joy, and death and apparent absorption in the soul of the universe ends the scene.